AF265169

DON'T FORGET TO SHINE

for women who need to put themselves first

LASHEERA LEE

Don't Forget to Shine: for women who need to put themselves first © 2019 La Sheera Lee.

ISBN: 976-0-9990126-6-1
Printed in the United States of America

All rights reserved. This book or any portion thereof may not be reproduced or used in any manner whatsoever without the express written permission of the publisher except for the use of brief quotations in a book review. No part of this publication may be reproduced, stored, in a retrieval system, copied in any means, electronic, mechanical, photocopying, or recording. No part of this book may be uploaded without permission from the author.

Read You Later Communications, LLC.
www.readyoulater.biz

ACKNOWLEDGMENTS

First, I would like to thank God for all making all things possible. Without his guidance, I would be nothing. I am grateful for my loving family. They inspire me to be my best. I have to give a shout out to the wonderful women of Round Table Readers Book Club and my Shine Sisters. They each encourage me in various ways. I want to thank the countless people who encourage me on social media. Your warm words of encouragement and laughs give a sister life.

Keep Shining.

COME HERE.

Yes, move a little closer. Do you know the real you?

Yes, I am talking to the woman who has hidden so many silent cries and shielded her pain from the eyes of the world.

Yes, I am talking to the courageous woman who constantly places herself last, so others will not feel threatened or neglected.

Honey, yes, I am speaking to you. The patient woman who wants to fly but is scared of leaving others behind. I am talking to the unstoppable woman who wants more out of life but is afraid of outshining her family and friends.

Yes! I am speaking to you.

You have lived your life in the shadows of other people thoughts, words and expectations. You went to the school your family wanted you to attend. You remain on a job you hate because you feel you have no recourse. Some of you even dated and married the wrong man because people told you it was the right thing to do.

You have lived your light in the glow of family, friends, and sad to say, acquaintances. The bible states:

It is better to take refuge in the Lord than to trust in man.

Psalm 118:8

I am not saying that you shouldn't seek wise counsel. However, you should trust what God is saying to YOU. Enter into a relationship with Him, where you know you are hearing and obeying His voice and His voice alone. Woman of purpose set yourself free.

You carry the battle scars of family, friends, and life in your mental space as a memento void of promises. Promises that were supposed to protect, love, conceal, and in some cases, even minister to the real woman you are.

Rarely, have you stopped to seek attention for these scars. You have allowed them to overlap with rejection, hardship, broken vows, etc. Therefore, they now have scar tissues that are riddled with so many disconnected elements, that is hard to recognize the reflection in your mirror.

The world only sees the whole woman you portray in public. Some of you have worn the scars so long, you believe that is a natural part of your existence. The Bible States:

Trust in the Lord with all your heart, and do not lean on your own understanding, acknowledge Him, and He will make straight your paths.

Proverbs 3:5-6

When you cast all; not some, but all of your problems on

His ear, it will free your mind, body, and soul. Those scars will dissolve and you will find peace. Woman of wisdom, claim your peace. Your careers, relationships, churches, organizations, and even marriages are based on seeking the approval of the people that are around you.

Essentially you enter into an unequally yoked covenant with yourself. Do your words line up with your actions? Are you blessing and cursing yourself at the same time? If so, you are joined with an unbeliever. You are sowing seeds of doubt in your own circumstances. Doubts can come from our own minds and heart.

Often, the devil uses our doubts to lay the foundation of fear, procrastination, and stagnation. In short, he wants to immobilize your steps. He does not want you to get to that next level. We know through scripture that Jesus references the devil as the Father of Lies. John 8:44.

He wants to plant seeds of discord in your head. Who best to sabotage your plans, then you? Often, we are so busy thinking people are plotting against us or not supporting us, that we fail to review our own actions. Are you responsible for plotting your own undermining?

Get out of your own way.

You don't respect yourself enough to ask yourself vital questions about your life and emotional stability. Respect that is unquestionably yours to have and behold. Woman of substance, it is time to take back your power.

You have been playing the side chick role to your own persona for far too long. You view your own life as a jump off. You place little time on your wants to appease others around you. You keep the good, bad, and, the ugly to yourself; You get use to receiving only little nuggets from the entire gold bar.

You tell yourself that you don't need or want more. All the

while, your heart and mind are yearning for quality and tranquillity. You place your feeling aside so you can enter into a realm of sub-consciousness, which does not allow you to think or feel.

You are like an actress on stage; reciting lines and plastering fake smiles for audiences. You are surviving, not living. You think by carrying the burdensome loads, you are doing the world a favor. Therefore, you walk around inwardly broken. Often not having the strength to cry for your own emotional demise.

Just like any other good side chick you make yourself available to everyone but yourself. You sleep with unbelievable sacrifice and wake up to bitterness. You dance with rejection and wake up to fear. You have placed your goodies in the hands of other people. You have allowed the most vulnerable parts of you to be open on full display.

Your values and beliefs are jaded by the negative experiences and how you have allowed yourself to be treated. You believe that by placing others first you are doing the honorable thing. You have mentally, physically, spiritually, and financially given until it hurts. What are you trying to do? Who are you trying to please? Woman of truth, it is time to live in your light.

As we enter into this journey of basking in our light. Don't be afraid to glow and strut your stuff. You have allowed your talents, personality, and greatness to be hidden for far too long. Get out your pen and paper. We are going on a trip that will allow you to enjoy life in the sunshine.

WHAT SIGNS ARE YOU READING?

IF YOU WERE GIVEN a task to describe your current life path via traffic signs, how would you proceed? Would your current road be full of yield signs, road under construction, exit closed, U-turn, do not enter, divided highway, sharp curves ahead, detour, stop sign, rest area, no parking, no U-turn, reserved parking, freeway entrance, green light, yellow light, look both ways.

Take a few minutes to write or highlight the top three road signs that describe your current life path. As a driver or a passenger, you know the road or signs often change pattern or courses. The signs allow you and others to be prepared for changes that lie ahead. It gets you mentally and physically prepared to enter into another space.

If you were on a road with no signs or no changes, you might feel alarmed. It might cause one to wonder if you are on the wrong course. As you advance, you will take on different paths and signs. The problem lies with so many of us, is that we feel one sign is applicable to all of our life transitions or situations.

You have endured betrayal in the past. Therefore, you have an exit closed sign around your heart and mind. It is never open to allow possibilities of what if's to occur. Are you missing out on valuable and nurturing relationships due to you wearing the wrong sign at the wrong time?

Betrayal often births bitterness. The seed of bitterness never cast valuable fruit. Bitterness will distort your mind and change the path of your life. Bitterness will make your cast clouds on a sunshiny day. Is your tongue so strong that you strike without thinking or reserve? What purpose are your acidic words or actions edifying? The Bible states:

The heart knows its own bitterness, and no stranger shares its joy.

Proverbs 14:10

You assert your bitterness like a badge of honor that provokes conflict, strife, and miscommunication. You might call it another element of keeping it real. However, if the sole purpose of your statements or actions are to shun everyone from yourself, how real are you?

You need to deal with the root of your bitterness. You can't heal, what you state does not exist It might not happen over time but you can revive your joy.

Exercise

Highlight or write the word or words from the list below, you feel are preventing you from moving on to a new sign in your life. After you have highlighted or written down the words on a sheet of paper, address what is the natural cause of this bitterness.

- Fear
- Procrastination
- Trust
- Communication
- Self-Acceptance
- Love
- Forgiveness
- Shame
- Mistrust
- Misplaced Loyalty

How are you going to use this information to move forward? Baby, you have to stop misplacing or utilizing the right signs at the wrong time. Your peace, mental health, and joy depends on you switching these lanes and turning these signals.

Over the years I have heard or been told that incidents that made me or others feel dejected were not "that bad."

Honey, don't allow anyone to place their stamp on your feelings. Now that does not mean you should wallow in self-pity, or make yourself your own personal poster child for defeat and neglect. However, use that energy to evoke positive changes in your life. Write down who you are, not what you were. Jot down new directions, don't focus on past indiscretions.

That being said, we need to own up to our messes, but our messes don't own us. There are times, we all ponder, Why? Why do we have to have to encounter heartaches, depression, abuse, and other misfortunes?

There are times, sisters, you might feel trapped, with no light at the end of the tunnel. Or the light you thought you saw, was a train barreling down the track. Know this, situations do change. Your words have power. Your prayers are heard. You will not remain in this stagnant state.

You will get up and get better. You are worthy of more than you imagine. The Bible states:

He has made everything beautiful in its time. He has also set eternity in the human heart; yet no one can fathom what God has done from beginning to end.

Ecclesiastes 3:11

The issue that set you back, will now set you up for success. Stop looking in the mirror to see what came for you. Grab a new road sign and enter onto your new freeway entrance. Woman of life, your road will have transitions. Potholes, detour signs, and sharp curves ahead might be on that path. Please don't allow the anger and resent, and hurt to fester into 10 bitter pills, that will only secure to choke your plans in the end.

IN CASE OF BAD WEATHER, SEEK SHELTER

How many of you were told as kids when the weather was bad to seek shelter? As a child, I was instructed to never stand outside, when it was lightning. I was also taught to cut off and unplug all electrical appliances during an electrical storm.

Admittedly, I thought the second lesson was too much to bare. The notion that lightning could damage something inside of a structure, was lost on a mind of an excited ten-year-old that wanted to watch The Jackson Five on television.

However, during my childhood, one never questioned adults, especially your grandma. Everyone in the South, growing up in the '70s and '80s, knew that whatever, I mean *whatever* Big Ma stated was law.

My grandmother was no exception to that rule. She took pride in physically and mentally nurturing anyone that was in her path. She would literally take the clothes off her back and food in our freezer to help anyone she "thought" was in need. Therefore by her virtue and actions, not words, she demanded and received respect. Some of you will catch that later.

I vividly recall one steamy summer evening, dark, brooding clouds were hovering over my grandmother's house, Heavy rains were pounding the roof, causing mud puddles to form around the house. The sky was lit with natural electricity making a presence.

The southern summer was hot and muggy. Honey, the kind of muggy that made you want to take three baths before noon. The streaks in the sky continued to have their own light show in the sky. It was accompanied by the loud bass of thunder clapping its hands.

My grandma yelled from the back of the house for me to fix the television. Sisters, this is my moment of truth. I stated earlier, that we have to own up to our mess. Well, I am telling you one of my truths. I knew what my grandma meant by stating "fix" the television. She wanted me to turn off and unplug the television.

However, in my precocious ten-year-old mind, I had a moment of slickness. I took it upon my hard-headed self to only turn off the television. In my mind, I knew that both turning off the television and unplugging the television was way too much. What did my grandmother know, right?

My grandmother walked down the narrow hall toward the cozy living room. She sat in her favorite gently used green Lazy Boy Recliner Chair. The chair was one of the few luxurious she afforded. Now, if you grew up with southern grandparents in the '70s and '80s you also know that you were not to sit in "that" chair that belonged to your elders. That was a huge no, no.

Several minutes after she sat down in her cozy chair, bolts lightning grazed the sky. We all sat in the hot living room. The only sounds that could be heard were the claps of thunder and heavy rains pouring down. All of sudden there was a light bolting in our front door. A streak of lightning came through our door. It meticulously made its way to our television sitting on the old console. You could see and hear the zapping noises being made, as the lighting and television entered into a tug of war. Of course, the lighting won the battle.

I sat there mesmerized at the occurrence. My eyes were huge from fright and fear. My feelings of fright were from if the lighting would zap me next. My fear was from the consequence I might suffer, from being disobedient. My grandmother slowly made her way to our now frayed television. She investigated the back of the model. Her eyes instinctively moved to the plug that was in the wall.

Next, her eyes followed a path to my fearful behind. I sat there in the chair frightened to move and too scared to utter a word. She carefully made her way back to her beloved chair and looked towards me. The words she uttered were soft but carried great meaning. She stated, *"Baby, when grandma tells you to do something, it is for a reason. I would never tell you to do something that will harm you. You will soon learn who to take shelter in."*

As a child, I did not fully understand the meanings of her words. Honestly, I was too fearful to ask too many questions. However, as an adult, I have come to recall those words on many occasions.

How often do we seek shelter in the wrong people, places, habits, or things? Many of us are willingly plugged into situations that are zapping us on a daily basis. When are you going to let go?

Are you scared that the shelter you seek is better than the unknown? Are you scared to leave your familiar place, due to the rocky passage you might encounter on your journey?

Life is all about the unknown.

That is generally what scares the heck out of most of us. It is also the reason why many of us remain in unstable shelters. The roof could be leaking, the foundation might be cracking, and the walls can feel like they are literally closing in on you.

However, you are scared to travel to the safety of a new shelter. You continue to yearn for that familiar relationship, situation, or job because—it is what you know. It is time for you to seek the safety of the sound shelter. You will have a hard task finding peace in an unsafe structure. The word states:

1 Whoever dwells in the shelter of the Most High will rest in the shadow of the Almighty. 2 I will say of the LORD, He is my refuge and my fortress, my God, in whom I trust. 3 Surely he will save you from the fowler's snare and from the deadly pestilence. 4 He will cover you with his feathers, and under his wings, you will find refuge; his faithfulness will be your shield and rampart. 5 You will not fear the terror of night, nor the arrow that flies by day, 6 nor the pestilence that stalks in the darkness, nor the plague that destroys at midday.

Psalms 91:1-6

Find that safe place to cast your burdens and care upon. The burdens you carry are not your only to hold. When you are truly able to let go, you will find peace. Peace when everything else around you looks like chaos.

At one point, I was dealing with a lot of things at one time. Honey, I was stressed. There was a situation on every corner, street, park, and avenue, A Sister Was Tired, folks. One evening as I was praying, I could not escape the word *peace*.

Often, we pray for God to resolve the situation. However, we forget to pray for Him to grant us peace during the situation. Some issues will not be solved quickly. Take rest in the fact that you have been granted access to peace. Think of it as your secret shield. It is an invisible force that protects you from harm.

I asked him for peace in all situations. That means I can't allow others to distress me with their issues. I am not saying don't be a concerned friend or listening partner. I am saying don't allow your peace to be disturbed. Protect your peace at all cost. It is a valuable asset. Regardless of what it looks like, you are blessed. Don't allow negative energy to rent a spot in your head.

SAVE SOME FOR YOU

She leaps over her emotions in a single bound. She hides her scars so that she might appear happy to the world. She negotiates her life based on the opinions, feelings, and needs of others.

She incredulously thinks, that without help, she is able to tackle all obstacles in her way. Who is this threadbare woman? She is the myth of the superwoman.

Have you ever had a cake or pie so good, that you instinctively knew, everyone else would want a piece. Therefore, before you would dig in, you will state, 'save some for me'. Honey, that should be your new motto, save some for me.

How much are yourself are you going to give away? Have you stopped to count up the cost? You are allowing the world too literally and figuratively eat you up. As women, we try to be everything to everyone.

Often we put our own needs and wants on the back burner. Ladies, there are consequences and repercussions for not taking care of ourselves. Save some for you. You are deserving of wonderful and great things. You are deserving to live a life fulfilled of blessings spoken over you. Your dreams and goals are attainable.

Learn to celebrate your milestones and accomplishments. Don't allow others to diminish any progress that you have made. Meaning—take charge of your life and do things that are satisfying, inspiring, and invigorating to your psyche.

Connecting the dots was a game I used to enjoy as a child. I used to enjoy getting to the next step. As an adult, connecting all of the dots can be a lot more challenging.

Often, we have to retrace our steps. At times we have to go around some dots. Honestly, there are times that you stopped playing because you felt lost or was too tired to continue, at the moment.

Sister, it is the time to get out your new pen and paper and start connecting your dots. You cannot win if you do not play. Does your ecosystem meet your new standard? Are you attempting to fish on dry land? Are you still trying to gather figs in a dessert?

An essential part of saving some for yourself is learning to navigate through the right ecosystem. If you are waiting for that perfect moment to launch your business, go on that trip, or enter into a relationship, baby you better reconsider your thought process.

Often, we are too busy living for others, to understand what we are purposed to perform. Pray about it. Write down your goals. Go for what you know. This year has been full of reminders that life is not a dress rehearsal. What are you waiting for?

Exercise

1. Write two things you are going to do for yourself this year.

2. Write steps you are going to take to make sure number one happens.

YOU ARE LIGHT

Brilliant flash. Dashing for them to view
Triumph Over her Insecurities, awaiting her new, new.
No longer willing to live in obscurity. Her boldness
dripping like sweet dew.
The world needs your light. So do you.

IF WE ARE HONEST, not everywhere we place our feet is a ray of sunshine. It is important that you have that inner glow of positivity pumping from your veins. Think of it as a time release capsule, pumping as needed.

When you go to places that you encounter a great deal of negativity, It is imperative that you bring your own dose of sunshine with you. Being discriminated against because your skin tone, gender, or religion, is not a new phenomenon in our society.

However, the current wave of hate and intolerance is a fact we can't ignore. Cover yourself in prayer. Align your mind in faith. Take action via voting and organizing. Delete toxic rhetoric and people that are making you depressed and physically sick.

Replace the negative words with positive love notes to yourself. You are gifted, beautiful, and smart. Love who you are. Don't allow the hatred displayed in the world today, make you display hate. Lead in love.

It is becoming increasingly clear that we as women, often embrace our roles as pain bearers to a grave degree. We birth nations, cultivate communities, sustain businesses, and serve our ministries. Yet, we are often deemed too emotional or not qualified to parent the babies we have birthed and nurtured.

We were only used for the painful task. We carry on our general lives with a smile, while we are crying inside. Often, our wounds are so deep, that we no longer outwardly bleed. Our wounds manifest as depression, self-doubt, poor relationships, and self-inflicted pain. The pain bearer you are, takes on more pain because that is what you are made to do, right?

Honey, even a luxury car needs to be recharged or replenished to run. What makes you think you can continue to run on the empty fumes of pain? You were created to enjoy life. Give yourself permission to enjoy all of what life has to offer. Please don't allow yourself to be manipulated by toxic situations and empty, self-serving sermons. Break free!

YOU ARE MORE than your setbacks, rejections, dismissals, or mistakes. Embrace your efforts. Stop carrying failed relationships, bad decisions, or errors into your current space. You need to love yourself enough to let your past go.

Forgive yourself. Forgiveness is necessary so that you want to ambush your purpose. The devil knows that if he can keep you in a woe is me state of mind, you will be less likely to set and meet your goals. It is not God's desire for you to live in your past. The Bible states:

Remember not the former things, nor consider the things of old. Behold, I am doing a new thing; now it springs forth, do you not perceive it? I will make a way in the wilderness and rivers in the desert.

Isaiah 43:18-19

It is His desire for you to live in freedom and wholeness. It will be hard for you to get free, dragging past baggage into your new situation. Guilt and shame our not your friends. They provoke memories that hold you hostage to dead things.

It is time for you to live your life without the shackles of the past. You are worthy of all good things headed in your direction. Don't self-sabotage your goals. Allow that uncomfortable situation to birth your purpose.

Use all the tools you encountered in the turmoil, to be a catalyst for your next stage of life. Honey, there is a lesson in everything. It is up to you to learn and grow from past setbacks.

Yes, you must grow from the errors. If you don't elevate your mind from these oversights, you might fall into the pattern of learning and repeat.

How many of you have sat in a class, listened to instruction, took down the notes, and failed the test? Why? You learned the lesson. However, you did not engage in strategies and use tools that would help you pass the test.

It is not enough to learn the lesson, you must be able to pass the test. Passing the test will prevent you from going on the merry go ride of learn and repeat. People who state they have learned their lesson but repeat the same pattern. It is time for you to move on from foolishness.

Elevate your mind with positive music, people, and words. Stop engaging in activities that remind you of bad memories or places. Lighten your load and let it go.

Exercise

1. Write down feeling, places, and events that have caused you to feel guilt or shame.

2. Place them in an envelope.

3. Ask God to release these feelings of negativity from your mind, body, and spirit.

4. Place the envelope in a trash can.

5. Take the trash immediately out of your house.

Releasing these emotions are a powerful entity. If you need to cry, cry. If you feel the need to scream, do it. Let these emotions go. It is important for these emotions to be released, so God can do His work. He wants you to live free and unencumbered. Allow Him to elevate you.

LET IT GLOW

SISTER, you are a work of art. Your cellulite, wrinkles, nose, lips, laugh, and sass are to all be treasured. Your beauty is not to be compared but admired. Your gifts are countless. Sister, you turn heads with your presence, wit, and charm.

Your ability to get up and show up is unparalleled to none. You have raised villages, placed politicians in offices, and built churches. Yet, you often don't receive the accolades you deserve.

Sister, I come to serve you notice, I appreciate and see monumental steps you take each day, Often, the world is not kind to you. They cast you in roles that are unfitting for your lineage. They place stereotypes on you that fit their fears. Yet, you rise up, like the queen you are, to meet and defeat, each roadblock headed your way.

You have endured tears and heartaches. You are often not heard or appreciated by the people you assist. However, you keep casting out the net to save others. Ladies, it is time to demonstrate some self-love.

Do you know the entire world, waits for you to introduce the next fashion trend? Your words are so powerful that people repeat them all over the world. Sisters, you are truly mesmerizing in every sense of the word. You laugh is contagious.

When you smile, you bring an entirely different atmosphere to the room. Your Sister Girl outings are legendary. The way you bound with your girls, is the stuff other people want. Every time my book club members have a meeting in a public place, there is always someone who states that want to come to our table. The love and good times we share can't be duplicated. There is nothing like being in the company of your sisters. Don't allow the world to tell you differently.

We can all win together. That is the power of being uplifted by a band of wonderful women. Women who don't have to encounter the same struggle to know the struggle. Sisters who understand the importance and essence of having your back. Sisters, you have sown good seeds in fertile ground. Now, it is your time to shine. Go forth and live the quality of life you were destined to behold, It is your life to live. Step out of the boxes that have contained your hidden gems. Don't forget to shine.

Daily Exercise
1. Start off each day with a prayer.
2. Say something positive about yourself.
3. Write yourself love notes to yourself
4. Plan. Plan. Plan. Jot down ideas, goals, and notes in your planner.
5. Take a few minutes each day to do something you like.
6. Don't go to bed with the weight of the world on your shoulders.

7. Engage in a relaxing activity before you enter your bedroom. Your bedroom should be your sanctuary. Make it a place of peace.

ABOUT THE AUTHOR

Award-winning blogger, La Sheera Lee, M.Ed., is a wife, mother, educator, podcaster, moderator, and author. She is on a mission to help others to see the beauty of their own voices. La Sheera, also known for her savvy role as a social media strategist and influencer, loves to help people connect the dots. She utilizes the power of social media to inspire, inform and educate on a global level. A native of a small city in Virginia, this Teacher of the Year, realizes that success is leading the next person forward. She is a sister who loves chocolate, a good book, and a nice beverage. You can hear her on: www.blogtalk.com/readyoulater; where your voice is heard. You can also connect with her at www.readyoulater.biz.

facebook.com/lasheera.lee

twitter.com/readyoulater

instagram.com/readyoulater

NOTES

NOTES

NOTES

NOTES

www.ingramcontent.com/pod-product-compliance
Lightning Source LLC
Chambersburg PA
CBHW061103050726
47592CB00004B/1808